1907	Birmingham acquires the three tapestries made for Compton Hall, 'The Arming & Departure', 'The Failure of Sir Gawaine', and 'The Attainment' for the city's collection, with the support of two hundred and fifty local subscribers, for £1000.
	Knox D'Arcy buys the cartoons for the Holy Grail tapestries from Morris & Co. to prevent any further versions being produced. After his death in 1917, his widow sells them back to the Firm.
1917	Tapestry workshops at Merton Abbey close as most weavers are on active service due to the First World War. They reopen in the 1920s.
1932	Versions of 'The Summons' and 'The Attainment are woven for Henry Beecham of Lympne Castle, Kent.
1940	Morris & Co. closes.
1941	Birmingham acquires a group of printed and woven textiles and designs from Morris & Co.'s showroom.
1947	Mrs Middlemore's daughter gives 'The Ship' and the 'Verdure' woven for Melsetter House to Birmingham's collection.
1980	Birmingham acquires 'The Summons' from the series commissioned by George McCulloch with the support of several major grant giving bodies and 19 trusts and supporters, for over £90,000.
1994	Birmingham makes an unsuccessful attempt to acquire 'The Failure of Sir Lancelot' from the series commissioned by George McCulloch at auction.

THE HOLY GRAIL TAPESTRIES

The Holy Grail tapestry series illustrates the story of the search for the Holy Grail by the Knights of the Round Table. It was conceived by William Morris and Edward Burne-Jones in 1890, and is widely regarded as one of the outstanding achievements of the British Arts and Crafts Movement.

This guide begins with the original Holy Grail Tapestries series, which was part of the interior decoration of Stanmore Hall in Middlesex, produced between 1890 and 1895. It goes on to consider each of the tapestries in Birmingham's collection, which were all later versions. It concludes with a look at the complex, collaborative process involved in their creation.

These six tapestries were acquired by the city between 1907 and 1980. They were produced by Morris & Co. for three different clients over a period of five years, from 1895 to 1900. Collectively, they are the most coherent and surviving representation of this series, and one of the enduring highlights of Birmingham's collection.

ORIGINAL COMMISSION
AT STANMORE HALL

The Holy Grail tapestry series represents both the culmination of William Morris's longstanding desire to revive the art of tapestry weaving, and the pinnacle of his artistic collaboration with his close friend, Edward Burne-Jones. In 1890, a major commission from William Knox D'Arcy to decorate and furnish his entire home, Stanmore Hall in Middlesex, provided Morris with the opportunity to realise his goal of creating a narrative series of tapestries on a grand scale. Morris was ambivalent about the client, who had made a substantial fortune as the Director of the Mount Morgan Goldmining Company, with mines in Australia and New Zealand. He was also disparaging about the architectural style of the house, which had been built relatively recently in 1847 and extended later.

Their literary source was Thomas Malory's 'Le Morte d'Arthur'. Written in the 15th century, it was reprinted in 1817 and a copy was discovered by Burne-Jones in a bookshop in New St, Birmingham in 1855. It was a book which both men cared about passionately, and returned to as subject matter for their work throughout their lives. In the comradeship of the knights and their heroic quest, they saw an allegory for their own artistic endeavours.

Images of the dining room at Stanmore Hall from The Studio magazine, 1899.

Opposite top left: 'The Summons' with verdures below

Opposite bottom left: 'The Arming & Departure', with verdures below

Above: 'The Failure of Sir Lancelot', with verdure below

Right: 'The Attainment', with tables and doorway below

Knox D'Arcy paid Morris & Co. a fee of £3,500 for twelve tapestries, £1,000 of which went to Burne-Jones for his designs. None of the tapestries in Birmingham's collection are from this original set, but the scale and design of the tapestries in Birmingham's collection derive from this original commission, woven between 1892 and 1895. The dimensions of the dining room and the particular placing of the windows, chimney breast, and built-in serving tables that ran along one wall determined the designers' approach. The subjects were conceived as a narrative series of six, to be hung between the cornice and the dado rail. Below four of the narrative subjects were verdure tapestries, with banner-style inscriptions that described the sequence of events taking place above. The figurative tapestries were therefore originally intended to be viewed from below, hung nearly two metres above the ground.

The text from these inscriptions, probably written by Morris himself, is featured beneath the title of each tapestry on the following pages of this guide.

THE HOLY GRAIL TAPESTRIES IN BIRMINGHAM'S COLLECTION

THE KNIGHTS OF THE ROUND TABLE SUMMONED TO THE QUEST BY THE STRANGE DAMSEL

'HOW KING ARTHUR SAT IN HIS HALL AT THE HIGH TIDE OF PENTECOST AND HOW THE WHOLE ROUND TABLE WAS THERE ASSEMBLED WHEN THERE ENTERED TO THEM A DAMSEL AND CALLED UPON THE KNIGHTS TO TAKE UPON THEM THE QUEST OF THE SANGREAL WHEREOF WAS GREAT STIR AND WONDER AMONGST THEM OF THE ROUND TABLE BOTH THE KING AND HIS KNIGHTS'

The first scene in the story shows a damsel appearing before King Arthur and the Knights of the Round Table, summoning them to undertake the quest for the Holy Grail. The Grail was the vessel that Christ drank from at the Last Supper, also said to have been used by Joseph of Arimathea to catch Christ's blood at the Crucifixion.

The main characters who feature later on are Sir Lancelot, who raises his hand, on the far left, and Sir Gawaine, wearing the blue robe, on the right.

In 1898-99, a set of narrative panels was woven for George McCulloch, who was a colleague of Knox D'Arcy's, for his house in Kensington, London. This version of the 'Summons' is from that set, acquired by Birmingham Museums in 1980.

The Arming and Departure of the Knights of the Round Table on the Quest for the Holy Grail

'HOW AFTER THE DAMSEL HAD BIDDEN THE KNIGHTS OF THE ROUND TABLE TO SEEK THE SAN GREAL THEY DEPARTED ON THE QUEST WHATEVER MIGHT BEFALL THAT OF THOSE THAT THUS DEPARTED THESE ARE THE CHIEFEST SIR GAWAINE, SIR LANCELOT OF THE LAKE, SIR HECTOR DE MARYS, SIR BORS DE GANYS, SIR PERCEVAL AND SIR GALAHAD'

This second narrative panel depicts the ladies of King Arthur's Court assisting the knights in preparation for their quest. On the far left, Queen Guinevere hands Sir Lancelot his shield, in an allusion to their adulterous relationship, the cause of Lancelot's impending failure. Sir Gawaine, who will also fail in the quest, appears mounted on the right of the picture, with his shield bearing a double-headed eagle. The costumes are loosely based on those of the twelfth century, and were probably taken from Henry Shaw's 'Dresses and Decorations of the Middle Ages', which was a popular source book on historical costume.

This version of the Arming and Departure is one of three of the Holy Grail tapestries commissioned from Morris & Co. by Laurence Hodson for the drawing room of his home, Compton Hall, near Wolverhampton. They were the second weaving of the subject, and were on the looms directly after the original set for Knox D'Arcy was finished, from 1895-96, just within Morris's own lifetime. All three are now in Birmingham's collection, acquired by public subscription in 1907.

Hodson had inherited a prosperous Wolverhampton brewery from his father and became a major patron of the Arts and Crafts Movement and of Morris in particular. He commissioned Morris & Co. to decorate his house, and owned a full set of volumes produced by the

Kelmscott Press set up by Morris in 1891. He is thought to have fallen into financial difficulty due to his investment in collecting, and had to sell his collection and the Hall in 1906.

Two hundred and fifty local subscribers supported the purchase of these three tapestries for Birmingham's collection, costing £1000 in 1907. Whitworth Wallis, the Museum's first Keeper of the Gallery, wrote about the relative merits of the different versions of the tapestries. He argued that Morris personally supervised the production of these three, being one of the last projects he worked on before he died in 1896, and that in quality they surpassed the original series woven for Stanmore Hall, and the series woven in 1898-99 for George McCulloch. Hodson was a personal friend of Morris, as well as a client. Wallis wrote that 'he (Morris) would never have allowed Mr Hodson to have anything but the very best.'

The Failure of Sir Gawaine

'HOW SIR GAWAINE AND SIR UWAINE
WENT THEIR WAYS TO SEEK THE
SANGREAL BUT MIGHT NO WISE
ATTAIN TO THE SIGHT OF IT BUT WERE
BROUGHT TO SHAME BECAUSE OF THE
EVIL LIFE THEY LED AFORETIME'

The Quest for the Holy Grail was a moral and spiritual journey, framed by Christian teachings, as well as a demonstration of bravery and physical strength. Malory's text tells the story of individual knights and their various adventures, battling with other knights, encountering strange beasts and mysterious ladies. These events often culminate in symbolic visions or dreams. Only the purest characters are worthy of attaining the Grail, and Burne-Jones chose to focus on moments of failure for the middle panels.

These two knights, Sir Gawaine and Sir Uwaine, failed in their quest because they had led sinful lives. This scene shows them being prevented from entering a ruined chapel by an angel. The brilliant light shining from within suggests the presence of the Holy Grail.

This is another one of the three tapestries commissioned by Laurence Hodson for Compton Hall (1895-6).

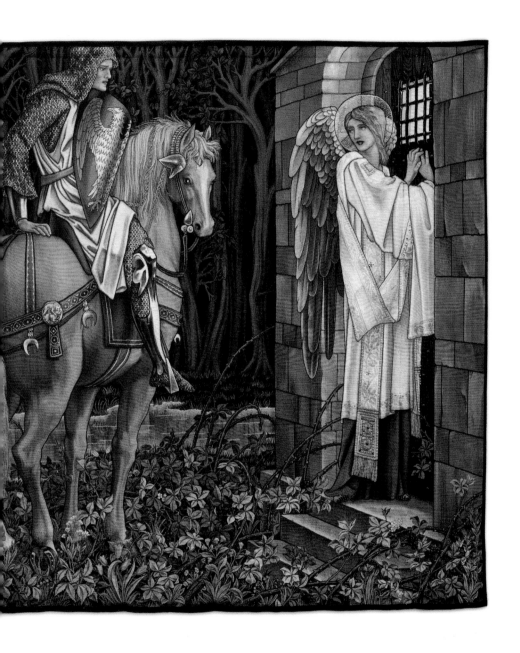

THE FAILURE
OF SIR LANCELOT

'OF THE QUEST OF
LANCELOT OF THE LAKE
AND HOW HE RODE THE
WORLD ROUND AND CAME
TO A CHAPEL WHEREIN
WAS THE SANGREAL BUT
BECAUSE OF HIS SINS HE
MIGHT NOT ENTER BUT FELL
ASLEEP BEFORE THE HOLY
THINGS AND WAS PUT TO
SHAME IN UNSEEMLY WISE'

This is the only narrative subject from the Holy Grail series which is not in Birmingham's collection. The tapestry illustrated here is from the third weaving commissioned by George McCulloch in 1898-9, the same set that 'The Summons' in Birmingham's collection was part of. It is now in a private collection.

Again, Burne-Jones's design shows the failed knight outside a chapel, looking as if he has fallen asleep, exhausted, as a bright light shines from within, and an angel stands in the doorway preventing his entry. The surrounding forest is dark and sinister, as a metaphor for the knight's moral and spiritual state. Lancelot was the strongest and most blessed of all the knights, until he betrayed King Arthur with his love for Queen Guinevere.

THE SHIP

Originally, this design was intended to fill an awkward space in the corner of the dining room at Stanmore Hall, without a verdure below, giving it a distinctive size and shape. It is an appropriate subject for the penultimate story panel. Ships were often used in medieval and classical sources as a narrative device to transport characters from one world to another, and they became a common visual motif of the Arts and Crafts Movement. In Malory's text the knights travelled by ship for part of their journey from Britain to Sarras, where the Grail was to be found.

This tapestry in Birmingham's collection was commissioned in 1900 by Mary Middlemore. Her husband, Thomas Middlemore, was a successful leather manufacturer based in Birmingham. The Middlemores were members of progressive circles in Birmingham and patrons of the Arts and Crafts. Mary was a keen embroiderer who had exhibited at Arts and Crafts exhibitions and knew May Morris, William Morris' daughter, who ran the embroidery workshops at Morris & Co. The Middlemores retired to Hoy in the Orkney Islands. Their home, Melsetter house, was designed by the architect W R Lethaby, and described by May Morris as 'A sort of fairy palace on the edge of the great northern sea'. This tapestry is thought to have been hung in the hallway. It was part of a group of tapestries donated to the Museum by Mrs Middlemore's daughter in 1947.

THE ATTAINMENT: THE VISION OF THE HOLY GRAIL TO SIR GALAHAD, SIR BORS AND SIR PERCEVAL

The original version of this subject hung above built-in serving tables and a doorway, so there were no verdure tapestries with inscriptions hung below it.

The final scene and culmination of the story is full of powerful Christian symbolism. Only three successful knights have been transported to the spiritual land of Sarras. Their relative distance from the Grail, which sits on the altar, relates directly to the purity of their lives. Furthest away stands Sir Bors, then Sir Perceval, and then Sir Galahad, who is the purest knight and most worthy of attaining the Grail. He kneels at the altar in prayer, surrounded by white lilies.

Between the men stand three angels, alluding to the Trinity. Two of them hold Eucharistic candles and the third carries the bleeding lance of Longinus, the Roman soldier who pierced Jesus's side on the Cross, and holds the dish of the Paschal Lamb, referencing the Last Supper. These symbols of Christ's Passion refer to the forgiveness of sins, the Resurrection, and the Sacrament of Communion. Above the Grail, a Pentecostal wind with drops of blood falling from it suggests the presence of the Holy Spirit.

All of the tapestry designs incorporate the dense, floral backgrounds inspired by medieval 'millefleurs' tapestries, which were added to Burne-Jones's designs by John Henry Dearle. Knox D'Arcy's gardener at Stanmore Hall identified all of the flowers, which are based on over thirty different native British plants, some of which would have grown locally on the banks of the River Wandle, which ran past the workshops at Merton Abbey. William Morris is said to have picked fresh flowers and given them to the weavers for reference.

This was the third of the tapestries commissioned by Laurence Hodson for Compton Hall (1895-6).

Verdure with deer and shields

A 'verdure' is a type of tapestry in which all or most of the pattern consists of leaves or trees, often with animals and flowers added. A 'millefleurs' or 'a thousand flowers' is a related type of pattern which developed in France and Flanders, and was common in the late Middle Ages. It depicted many different European flowers with botanical accuracy, either on their own or as the background for figurative designs.

Morris particularly admired late medieval tapestries which inspired and influenced his approach to design, as well as the technique and materials used to create the textiles produced by Morris & Co.

This Verdure, from Birmingham's collection was another of the two tapestries commissioned by Mary Middlemore in 1900, for Melsetter House. It was adapted from William

Morris's original designs by John Henry Dearle, after Morris's death. It is an amalgam of those that hung below the original narrative subjects in Stanmore Hall, and the banner reads as an introduction to the overall story and main characters. The shields were the only element of the series that Morris designed himself, with the devices derived from two 16th century French texts that he consulted in the British Museum. Each one represents a different knight. Sir Gawaine's, the double-headed eagle, Sir Lancelot's, the red diagonal stripes on a white background, and Sir Galahad's, the red cross on a white background, are prominently displayed.

DESIGN PROCESS

William Morris intended to revive the art of tapestry weaving in England. The process by which the various elements of the designs were combined and transferred to the loom was a complex one with several stages.

There are many drawings and studies surviving in public and private collections relating to the Holy Grail tapestries, but it is not always entirely clear which part of the process of production they relate to. They include rough composition sketches, studies of individual heads and figures, more finished drawings with body colour, and larger photographic cartoons.

Sketchbook,
Edward Burne-Jones,
about 1890, pencil and
coloured chalks.

Sketchbook, Edward Burne-Jones, about 1890, pencil.

One of Burne-Jones's sketchbooks in Birmingham's collection dates from about 1890-91 and shows some of his initial ideas and sketches relating to the series. It is full of visual references to historical precedents including Byzantine architecture, dress and decorative detail.

Several of the pencil sketches relate directly to elements in 'The Attainment' including this drawing of a historic chalice which Burne-Jones used as the model for the Holy Grail. His notes reference a history of German art published in Berlin in 1888, which illustrates the 8th century 'Tassilo Chalice' in the Kremsmünster Abbey in Austria. There are also early studies of boats, which evolved into the design for 'The Ship'.

Study for The Summons, about 1890, E Burne-Jones,
pencil, chalk, wash and bodycolour (51x103cm)

Study for The Attainment, E
Burne-Jones, about 1890-91,
watercolour, bodycolour, gum
and gold paint over traces of
pencil (51.6 x 159.3cm)

Two studies by Burne-Jones in Birmingham's collection from about 1890-91 show subsequent stages of the design process. 'The Summons' shows the overall composition with the figures in place, but has little detail and hardly any colour. By comparison, 'The Attainment' shows a much later stage with more details and colour added, but the flowers in the foreground and other decorative elements are missing.

The high level of decorative detail present in the final woven versions of the tapestries was provided by John Henry Dearle, who added to the drawings that Burne-Jones supplied to Morris & Co., and passed them back to him for comment or alteration. Tracings and enlarged photographs were used to eventually combine all the design elements into a working cartoon, which the weavers could refer to. The final stage before the weaving itself began was when the weavers transferred the outline design onto the individual warp threads on the loom, using a sharp piece of ivory dipped in ink.

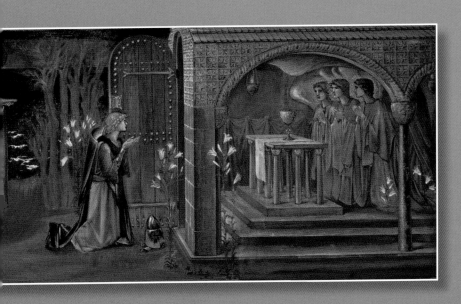

TAPESTRY WEAVING

Traditionally, tapestries provided warmth, decoration and were a practical form of wall covering, which could be rolled up and moved relatively easily. This type of heavy, hand-woven fabric depicting decorative and historic scenes was an important element of domestic interiors across Europe. Centres of production like Arras and Lille in France, and Brussels in Belgium were established from the 12th century onwards. However, by the end of the 18th century this tradition had declined, as fashion and taste changed, and there was a growing preference for patterned wallpaper or hanging pictures on plainer walls.

Tapestry weaving requires a large space, so it wasn't until Morris & Co's production moved to Merton Abbey in 1881 that Morris was able to set up three looms and begin training apprentices, inspired by the model of a medieval workshop. John Henry Dearle was his first apprentice, and he went on to become the workshop supervisor as well as a designer, and

Detail of the back of 'The Summons' in Birmingham's collection: The chairs and floral foreground.

Detail of the back of 'The Summons' in Birmingham's collection: The 'damsel'.

took over as manager of Merton Abbey after Morris died. All the weavers were young boys whom Morris thought had 'small, flexible fingers'. Morris chose to adopt the 'haut lisse' or 'high warp' method used in Arras and other medieval centres. This meant that the warp threads were arranged vertically rather than horizontally, with no limit on the width of the work produced. Three weavers could work alongside each other at each loom, at any one time. They sat behind the warp threads, and wove sideways, with the cartoon placed behind them. Opposite them were mirrors which reflected their progress from the front.

These fascinating details of the back of 'The Summons' tapestry in Birmingham's collection show the side that the weavers worked from. The design is reversed and the ends of the threads are visible.

Linda Parry, the leading expert on Morris textiles, has identified eleven tapestry weavers who were employed by Morris & Co. between 1890 and 1900, the period during which the tapestries in Birmingham's collection were produced: William Knight, William Sleath, John Martin, George Priestley, Robert Ellis, John Keech, William Haines, William Elliman, Walter Taylor, George Merritt, and John Glassbrook. Weavers were paid an

Detail of the back of 'The Summons' in Birmingham's collection: Sir Gawaine and others seated at the table.

average of £2.5s per square foot (930 square cm) of tapestry woven.

In tapestry weaving, designs are formed by filling threads, which are interlaced back and forth through the warp threads where required, rather than running completely across the full width of the fabric. All of the Holy Grail tapestries are made up of a cotton warp, with wool and silk weft threads, and some use of mohair and camel hair. There are between twelve and fourteen threads to the inch. These different types and colours of yarn were wound on to bobbins, which hung down at the back of the work. The shiny, reflective silks have been used effectively to depict shimmering light, rich fabrics, armour and other highlights, and the coarser animal hair adds texture to the coats of the deer and horses.

As well as providing more space, the facilities at Merton Abbey and the river nearby also gave Morris increased control over the dyeing process, and all the colours are derived from natural dyes produced on the premises.

GLOSSARY

Cartoon
A preparatory drawing for an art work in another medium, such as a painting, tapestry or stained glass window.

Christ's Passion
In Christianity, the Passion is the short final period in the life of Jesus, from his entry into Jerusalem to his execution by crucifixion.

Communion or Eucharist
The chief Sacrament and central act of Christian worship. Jesus Christ blessed bread and wine at the Last Supper with the words 'This is my body' and 'This is my blood'. Holy Communion is the act of receiving consecrated bread and wine.

Cornice
A decorative moulding running horizontally around the interior of a room, at the top of the walls, below the ceiling.

Cotton
Fibres derived from the cotton plant.

Dado
A rail running horizontally around the interior of a room, originally intended to protect the walls from damage caused by contact with the back of chairs.

Holy Grail
The vessel that Christ drank from at the Last Supper, said to have been used by Joseph of Arimathea to catch Christ's blood at the Crucifixion.

Kelmscott Press
Printing press established by William Morris in 1891.

Merton Abbey Works
The premises on a seven-acre site near Wimbledon, London where Morris & Co. established factory production in 1881, including tapestry weaving, textile dyeing and printing workshops.

Millefleurs
Literally 'a thousand flowers', a tapestry pattern depicting flowers with a high level of botanical accuracy, developed in France and Flanders and common in the late Middle Ages.

Pentecost
Also known as Whit Sunday, Pentecost is an important feast day in the Christian calendar. It takes place fifty days after Easter Sunday, and marks the day when the Holy Spirit came down among the Apostles.

Silk
Fibres produced from the cocoons of caterpillars, which are fine, strong and shiny, often used for their aesthetic appeal.

Tapestry
A heavy, handwoven fabric depicting historic or decorative scenes, used for wall hangings.

Verdure
A tapestry in which all or most of the pattern consists of leaves or trees, often with flowers and animals added.

Warp threads
The threads that run lengthways in a woven fabric. They are held in parallel and under tension on a loom. In tapestry weaving the designs are formed by the weft threads, which are interlaced back and forth through the warp.

Wool
Fibres from the fleece of sheep or other animals: strong, versatile and often used for textiles that provide warmth.

PE⊙PLE

Arts and Crafts Movement

William Morris was one of the pioneers of this Movement in Britain, which spanned the late 19th to early 20th centuries. These architects, artists, designers and craftspeople were influenced by the ideas of John Ruskin. They challenged the social consequences of industrial manufacture, revived traditional skills and techniques, and aimed to raise standards of design.

Sir Edward Burne-Jones (1833–1898)

Painter born in Birmingham. Burne-Jones and Morris met whilst students at Exeter College, Oxford and became lifelong friends. A founder member of Morris & Co., Burne-Jones produced designs for stained glass, tapestry and book illustrations for the Kelmscott Press that Morris established in 1891.

John Henry Dearle (1859-1932)

The first apprentice tapestry weaver taught by Morris. He became supervisor of the tapestry workshop, designed textiles and wallpaper, was lead designer and manager at Merton Abbey, and became artistic director of the Firm after Morris died.

William Morris (1834–1896)

Artist, designer, novelist, poet, printer, founder of the Socialist League and Society for the Protection of Ancient Buildings, William Morris was an extraordinarily productive and influential figure whose legacy continues into the 21st century.

Morris, Marshall, Faulkner & Co. or 'The Firm' (1861-1940)

Business set up in 1861 by William Morris and a group of like-minded artists who aimed to raise standards in decorative art and design. In 1875 it became Morris & Co. under Morris's sole ownership. It catered for all aspects of interior design and produced stained glass, textiles, metalwork and furniture.

Dimensions of tapestries in Birmingham's collection (height followed by length)

The Summons (1980 M 60): 245 x 535 cm
The Arming and Departure (1907 M 129): 244 x 362 cm
The Failure of Sir Gawaine (1907 M 130): 243 x 296 cm
The Ship (1947 M 52): 241 x 130 cm
The Attainment (1907 M 131): 245 x 693 cm
Verdure with Deer and Shields: (1947 M 53): 156 x 318 cm

All the tapestries are woven on a cotton warp with wool, silk, camel hair and mohair weft threads.

FURTHER READING

Oliver Fairclough and Emmeline Leary, *Textiles by William Morris and Morris & Co. 1861-1940*, Thames & Hudson, 1981

Fiona McCarthy, *William Morris*, Faber & Faber, 1994

Fiona McCarthy, *The Last Pre-Raphaelite, Edward Burne-Jones and the Victorian Imagination*, Faber & Faber, 2012

Linda Parry, *William Morris Textiles*, V&A, 2013

Stephen Wildman and John Christian, Edward Burne-Jones, *Victorian Artist-Dreamer*, Metropolitan Museum of Art, New York, 1998

Pre-Raphaelite and Other Masters, The Andrew Lloyd Webber Collection, Royal Academy of Arts, 2003

PICTURE CREDITS

ACKNOWLEDGMENTS

Zelina Garland is Curatorial & Exhibitions Manager at Birmingham Museums Trust. She was previously Curator of Applied Art, responsible for Birmingham's textiles and dress collection.

The content of this guide is based on two previous publications by former curators: *The Holy Grail Tapestries Designed by Edward Burne-Jones for Morris & Co.* by Emmeline Leary for Birmingham Museums & Art Gallery, 1985 and *The Holy Grail Tapestries designed by Edward Burne-Jones, William Morris and J H Dearle for Morris & Co.* by Helen Proctor for Birmingham Museums & Art Gallery, 1997.

William Morris Textiles by Linda Parry, V&A, 2013 was an authoritative source of additional information.